A Preview of
Jesus's
Seminal Teachings
and Leadership

Isaac Kinuthia

ARCHWAY
PUBLISHING

Scripture taken from the Holy Bible, NEW INTERNATIONAL
VERSION®. Copyright © 1973, 1978, 1984, 2011 by Biblica,
Inc. All rights reserved worldwide. Used by permission. NEW
INTERNATIONAL VERSION® and NIV® are registered trademarks
of Biblica, Inc. Use of either trademark for the offering of goods
or services requires the prior written consent of Biblica US, Inc.
Archway Publishing books may be ordered
through booksellers or by contacting:

Archway Publishing
1663 Liberty Drive
Bloomington, IN 47403
www.archwaypublishing.com
1 (888) 242-5904

Because of the dynamic nature of the Internet, any web
addresses or links contained in this book may have changed
since publication and may no longer be valid. The views
expressed in this work are solely those of the author and do
not necessarily reflect the views of the publisher, and the
publisher hereby disclaims any responsibility for them.

Any people depicted in stock imagery provided
by Thinkstock are models, and such images are
being used for illustrative purposes only.
Certain stock imagery © Thinkstock.

ISBN: 978-1-4808-3697-6 (sc)
ISBN: 978-1-4808-3698-3 (e)

Library of Congress Control Number: 2016915578

Print information available on the last page.

Archway Publishing rev. date: 09/22/2016

A Tribute to Jesus and His Teachings

At the age of sixty-six, my father, Samuel, an ordained church elder, was detained (family detention) for nine months due to an unfortunate, unintentional, obscure error in seeking continuous relief. He applied to his detention situation the teaching of Jesus: that people ought to pray. He made two collect phone calls, one in the morning and one in the evening, from his detention facility every day for the nine months he was detained, to pray with his family (my mother, Naomi; my brother, Stephen; and my sister, Jacqueline). He credits this as one of the things that helped him survive this traumatic, agonizing family detention experience.

Jesus has influenced or inspired me the most. At age six almost thirty years ago, my life's perspective revolved around, helping my parent's rear two pigs, raise a couple dozen chickens, herding three goats and a sheep. A transition to education, learning or even writing about Jesus's seminal teachings and leadership was unimaginable. Jesus is the leader who gives voice and good news (Luke 4:18) to the poor.

CONTENTS

CHAPTER 1

JESUS INTRODUCED

We all listen to what presidents, musicians, actors, teachers, coaches, politicians, judges, and many other people have to say. Jesus is the only person to have predicted his death and be resurrected from the dead; hence, it's prudent or good to know what he said, and this book helps with that. This book aims to be a quick elevator pitch of Jesus's seminal teachings, an empowering knowledge for all nations. For Jesus scholars and enthusiasts, it can be a refreshment course for continued enrichment. It can also reinforce and help Jesus's followers absorb some of Jesus's familiar teachings. As an introduction for people not familiar with Jesus and his works, it can be an introductory preview to help generate a feeling of familiarity with his teachings for their own personal knowledge and empowerment. It may also help organize one's curiosity in advance of experiencing the entire Bible.

Jesus, also referred to as Jesus of Nazareth or Jesus Christ, is arguably the most influential person of all time, directly affecting over three billion people. Jesus did not and does not force people to follow him. His teachings do not ask his followers to force other people to follow him, and neither do his teachings ask his followers to punish or kill those who do not accept or follow him. He is worshipped as Christ by close to two billion Christians, and he is referred to as a prophet by close to a billion people from other religions. He is the only thirty-something to be willingly followed by this many people; it is thus fitting to learn from and study some of Jesus's teachings because they reflect beliefs that have influenced many.

Jesus's birth and death are celebrated and observed almost all over the world in many forms. Jesus's birthday is celebrated or observed on December 25, or Christmas Day. It is recorded that God sent the angel Gabriel to Nazareth, a town in Galilee, to speak to a virgin named Mary. Mary was pledged to be married to a man named Joseph, a descendant of David, and Gabriel was going to inform her that she had found favor with God. Furthermore, he told her that she would be with child and give birth to a son, and that she was to give the child the name Jesus. Jesus would be great and would be called the son of the Most High (Luke 1:26–33). The news of Jesus's birth is also recorded as having been spread out or proclaimed by an angel (Luke 2:9–13). It is also noted that there was a star that appeared in the sky to guide some wise men to Jesus's birth location (Matt. 2:1–2), and it is recorded that an insecure King Herod, in an attempt to kill baby Jesus, ordered the killing of all male children born at that time period (Matt. 2:16). These accounts of Jesus's birth appear to undercut the modern-day minimization of Jesus's divinity. If indeed angels announced Jesus's birth, then Jesus's claim of being the son of God can't just be dismissed so quickly.

Jesus's death is commemorated every spring on Good Friday, and his resurrection is observed that same weekend on Easter Sunday.

We know that Jesus was an incredible and visionary leader, especially given the humble beginnings of his ministry. Jesus did not trivialize the incremental increase of his ministry. He chose twelve men, whom he named his disciples, and by all accounts we know that they were not well-educated men—some of them were merely fishermen by profession. These would be the men Jesus used to launch his ministry. He spent three years with them, inspiring and commissioning them to teach what he had taught them. These disciples were responsible for pioneering Christianity as we know it today.

Jesus intended his message and teaching to be for all nations. Jesus instructed his disciples to go and make disciples of all nations (Matt. 28:19), hence the title reference of this book. Jesus wanted his teachings to reach people of all walks of life and all nations, regardless of their religions. The term Christianity was coined in Antioch as a reference to Jesus's disciples (Acts 11:26). Confining Jesus's teachings to a singular religion muddles his universality; his teachings are intended to cross both religions and cultures. Jesus showed that the enemy of humanity is not other people or religions, but Satan and his evil spirits (Matt. 12:43–45). Jesus's teachings are thus not for attacking or competing with other religions or other people. Jesus's teachings on Satan and his evil spirits show that his message went far beyond being a contrast with other religions; thus, Jesus's messages and teachings are knowledge that can be empowering for all people, and as we know, knowledge is power.

This book will attempt to speak in more detail about the following seminal teachings of Jesus.

- Jesus taught he was Lord.
- Jesus taught that he is the son of God, Christ, the Messiah, and savior of the world—and that he is more than a prophet.
- Jesus believed, affirmed, and quoted scriptures (the Bible).
- Jesus taught that heaven exists.
- Jesus believed in the Holy Spirit and the Holy Trinity.

- Jesus wanted people to believe in him.
- Jesus believed and affirmed the creation account.
- Jesus believed in the Ten Commandments and commanded people to love and be merciful.
- Jesus taught that divorce is breaking a commandment.
- Jesus affirmed the sanctity of life and affirmed that babies in the womb have life and feelings.
- Jesus believed in prayers, taught how to pray, and want people to pray.
- Jesus taught that evil spirits exist and gave insights on how evil spirits operate to ruin people's lives.
- Jesus taught that the world will come to an end, and he spoke of his second coming.
- Jesus did not condone sexual immorality, and he taught that there will be a judgment day and an afterlife.
- Jesus warned of false prophets and of persecutions of his followers.

Finally, this book will include widely quoted maxims of Jesus that are important to know, and it will offer a Bible disclosure and conclusion.

CHAPTER 2

JESUS TAUGHT HE WAS LORD

Jesus referred himself as Lord when he sent his disciples to get a donkey for him to ride on: "If anyone asks you, 'Why are you doing this?' say, 'The Lord needs it'" (Mark 11:3).

Jesus claimed to be Lord and above the Ten Commandments; this is why he did not need to observe the Sabbath: "For the Son of Man is Lord of the Sabbath" (Matt. 12:8).

Jesus equated hating him to hating God: "Whoever hates me hates my Father as well" (John 15:22–23).

Jesus declared that he owned everything that God owns, and that he has been granted authority over all people: "All I have is yours and all you have is mine" (John 17:10). "For you granted him authority over all people" (John 17:2; see also John 16:15).

Jesus taught that he would rise from the dead in three days, indicating that he had power to resurrect, power over death, and power over life: "And the Son of Man will be delivered over to the chief priests and the teachers of the law. They will condemn him to death and kill him. Three days later he will rise" (Mark 10:33–34). This teaching has garnered criticism and has been the focus of a lot of discussion today. This seems to intrigue some modern-day skeptics and critics who have wanted to undercut the message of Jesus. The truth of Jesus's death and resurrection form the basis of what Jesus's followers believe. This book attempts to speak to this truth, because Jesus showed that people can be resurrected and that this idea is not as far-fetched as critics and other religions would like to insinuate. In the transfiguration account, three of Jesus's disciples witnessed Jesus talk to Elijah and Moses (Matt. 17:4, 9, 12). In this account of the transfiguration, Moses and Elijah are seen speaking with Jesus. Scriptures record that Moses and Elijah lived hundreds of years before Jesus walked on the earth. Jesus affirmed the transfiguration conversation that ensued, indicating that Elijah did come; he also affirmed that the two people the three disciples saw talking with Jesus were indeed Elijah and Moses. This transfiguration account shows that people can in fact be resurrected, and three of Jesus's disciples were eyewitnesses. Scriptures record that Moses indeed died (Deut. 34), and Elijah is recorded as having ascended to heaven without dying (2 Kings 2).

Both men lived many centuries before Jesus's time on earth, so the account of Jesus's resurrection cannot be dismissed.

Jesus remade and changed the course of history by instituting that forgiveness of sin was now through his death and his blood of the covenant at the cross; no longer would sins need to be forgiven through animal sacrifice. The entire world's religions owe this absence of sacrifices in religious rituals today to Jesus: "Jesus took bread, and when he had given thanks, he broke it and gave it to his disciples, saying, 'Take and eat; this is my body.' Then he took a cup, and when he had given thanks, he gave it to them, saying, 'Drink from it, all of you. This is my blood of the covenant, which is poured out for many for the forgiveness of sins'" (Matt. 26:26–28).

Jesus taught that he is the way, the truth, and the life, and that no one can come to the Father except through him: "Jesus answered, 'I am the way and the truth and the life. No one comes to the Father except through me'" (John 14:6). This teaching has been the subject of debate in many religious circles. This book attempts to discuss the fact that Jesus is the only one recorded to have contended with and overcome the devil and the devil's temptations—fame, power, lust, and a call to worship other idols to test God (Matt. 4:1–11). Overcoming Satan is not a small feat. I confess that I have tried myself to overcome sin and have fallen short on many occasions. Scripture indicate Jesus was "the perfect lamb of God" that had no sin (2 Cor. 5:21), for him to qualify to wash away all mankind sins through his death on the cross (Matt. 26:26–28). We all can agree that being sinless or overcoming all sins is an extraordinary achievement, because we can recall instances where we have fallen short. Jesus is thus the perfect one to lead humanity and guide humanity to God, and his words saying that he is the only way to the father has some weight to them. Jesus has no track record of sin. This should count for and inspire confidence that he can show all humanity the way to God, whom almost all religions agree is holy. Respectfully, there been no other religion that has put forward a superior case than the achievements and teachings of Jesus, and so credit has to be given to Jesus as the most influential of all time.

Jesus is the leader who empowers.

CHAPTER 3

JESUS TAUGHT THAT HE IS THE SON OF GOD, CHRIST, THE MESSIAH, SAVIOR OF THE WORLD, AND MORE THAN A PROPHET

Jesus explicitly referred to himself as the son of God during his prayers. "After Jesus said this, he looked toward heaven and prayed: 'Father, the hour has come. Glorify your Son, that your Son may glorify you'" (John 17:1).

Jesus taught that he is the only son of God, sent by God to save the world, and that whoever believes in him will have eternal life. Jesus also indicated God loves him and has placed everything in his hands: "For God so loved the world that he gave his one and only Son, that whoever believes in him shall not perish but have eternal life ... For God did not send his Son into the world to condemn the world, but to save the world through him" (John 3:16–17). "The Father loves the Son and has placed everything in his hands" (John 3:35).

Jesus was called a prophet by a Samaritan women at a well, and he was not troubled at being called a prophet: "Sir," the woman said, "I can see that you are a prophet" (John 4:19). Jesus wanted to clarify that he was more than a prophet, and in fact he was the Messiah: "The woman said, 'I know that Messiah' (called Christ) 'is coming. When he comes, he will explain everything to us.' Then Jesus declared, 'I, the one speaking to you—I am he'" (John 4:25–26). Thus Jesus today would like to be referred to as Christ the Messiah by all other religions.

Jesus accepted the charge and did not renounce that he was the son of God to avoid death. When the Jewish leaders insisted Jesus must die because he had broken the law by claiming to be the son of God, "The Jewish leaders insisted, 'We have a law, and according to that law he must die, because he claimed to be the Son of God'" (John 19: 7). The Jewish leaders who lived at the time of Jesus testified that Jesus claimed be the son of God, and it was for this reason that Jesus was put to death. To show more respect to Jesus, all religions should state that Jesus died because he accepted the charge he was the son of God.

A crowd that heard Jesus testified for our benefit today that Jesus was the savior of the world: "Now we have heard for ourselves, and we know that this man really is the Savior of the world" (John 4:42).

Jesus explained he was a king, was not from this world, and had knowledge of his coming prior to coming. His reason for coming to this world was to testify the truth, to do the will of God, and to finish his work: "You are a king, then!" said Pilate. Jesus answered, "You say that I am a king. In fact, the reason I was born and came into the world is to testify to the truth." (John 18:37). "My food," said Jesus, "is to do the will of him who sent me and to finish his work" (John 4:34).

Jesus's teaching that he is the Lord, the Messiah, and the son of God (John 4:25–26) is very profound. Only Jesus has ever taught this. It is a profound thing to claim to be Lord, to claim to be the way, the truth, and the life. Jesus goes further to insist that he is the only way to the father. He claims he owns everything God owns, implying everything belongs to God—a reference to creation. He predicted that he would be killed, and that he would resurrect form the death in three days. All this sets Jesus apart, demonstrating much authority, insight, and confidence in what he is teaching. Jesus goes further and exercises due care, making sure he clarified that he is Lord, Messiah, and the son of God for our benefit, so that there is no doubt.

Respectfully, many religions today only go as far as prescribing morals and virtue, asking their followers to follow on a promise all will be well in the end. There is not a figure like Jesus, in all other religions, teaching such profound teachings. This profound teaching sets Jesus apart from all other religions founders or prominent figures. It is also worth noting and remembering that Jesus was about thirty years old and taught his teachings within a span of three years. This is quite a feat, not only because we know Jesus was about thirty years old when he began his ministry (Luke 3:23), but also because we now know his ministry's universality and growth, and we can appreciate his achievement. What thirty-year-old speaks like that?

Jesus is the leader who doesn't bamboozle.

Chapter 4

Jesus Believed, Affirmed, and Quoted Scriptures (the Bible)

The first five books (Genesis, Exodus, Leviticus, Numbers, and Deuteronomy) of the bible are credited to Moses.

Jesus validates Moses by indicating that the action by Moses of lifting a snake in the wilderness was prophesying Jesus being lifted up on the cross: "just as Moses lifted up the snake in the wilderness, so the Son of Man must be lifted up" (John 3:14).

Jesus affirmed scriptures and quoted Moses: "But in the account of the burning bush, even Moses showed that the dead rise, for he calls the Lord 'the God of Abraham, and the God of Isaac, and the God of Jacob.'" (Luke 20:37–38). By Jesus quoting this scriptural account of Moses, he also validated Abraham, Isaac, and Jacob as the fathers of faith. Other religions have sought to validate Ishmael rather than Jacob, but Jesus did not speak to this. Jesus also clarified that marriage is for this earth and that there are no marriages in the afterlife. This is against those who believe that there are virgin women offered as reward in the afterlife, if one dies in the act of conducting terror.

Jesus accepted and explained Moses's law, there by validating commandments and laws issued by Moses: "Some Pharisees came and tested him by asking, 'Is it lawful for a man to divorce his wife?' They said, 'Moses permitted a man to write a certificate of divorce and send her away.' It was because your hearts were hard that Moses wrote you this law," (Mark 10:2–5).

Jesus respected and didn't declare error in the scriptures: "None has been lost except the one doomed to destruction so that Scripture would be fulfilled" (John 17:12). Some folks in science or other religions have tried to argue that the Bible has errors.

Jesus validated scriptures when he taught that David inspired, by the Holy Spirit, prophesied about Jesus being the Messiah. "He asked, 'Why do the teachers of the law say that the Messiah is the son of David?' David himself, speaking by the Holy Spirit, declared: "'The Lord said to my Lord: "Sit at my right hand until I put your enemies under your feet."'"" (Mark 12:35–37). In this account, Jesus taught that the Holy Spirit inspires people and has been there since the time of David, who lived several hundred years before Jesus. David was the second king of Israel.

Jesus affirmed Noah and the flood account, where all were destroyed but Noah was saved in the ark: "Just as it was in the days of Noah, so also will it be in the days of the Son of Man. People were eating, drinking, marrying and being given in marriage up to the day Noah entered the ark. Then the flood came and destroyed them all. It was the same in the days of Lot. People were eating and drinking, buying and selling, planting and building. But the day Lot left Sodom, fire and sulfur rained down from heaven and destroyed them all" (Luke 12:26–29, 32). In this text, Jesus also affirmed scripture reference of Lot and Sodom, and he quoted these accounts. Jesus equated the Noah and Sodom accounts as a generation's failure to heed to warning of pending doom punishment for sins. Jesus further likened today's activities of eating, drinking, buying and selling, planting and building, and marrying and being given in marriage as distractions hindering people from heeding to the gospel's warnings.

This account of Noah, where all were destroyed by flood but Noah was saved in the ark (Luke 12:26–29, 32), has garnered critics from modern social culture and elites claiming that it is not possible. Critics argue that rainfall falling forty days and nights (Genesis 7:12) cannot destroy the whole world, but those in the United States familiar with Hurricanes Katrina and Sandy can attest to the devastating and heavy loss of property and life from heavy torrential rainfall for just a few days. Jesus affirmed Noah's account, where rainfall was directed to destroy (Gen. 7:11), unlike an unfortunate city stricken or in the path of a hurricane. Jesus is a trusted authority, so we cannot discount this account of Noah.

Jesus affirmed Elijah and Moses, indicating that they once lived in the past, have reappeared and talked with him, and are alive somewhere else: "Peter said to Jesus, 'Lord, it is good for us to be here. If you wish, I will put up three shelters—one for you, one for Moses and one for Elijah.' Jesus instructed them, 'Don't tell anyone what you have seen, But I tell you, Elijah has already come, and they did not recognize him'" (Matthew or Matt 17:4, 9, 12).

Another point of difference between Jesus and other religions that has been scrutinized is the idea of Jesus being more than a prophet. Other religions have challenged this, but when we connect that some notable prophets accepted by these other religions examples—Prophet Jonah, Elijah, Moses, David—all affirm and reference Jesus in some way or form. That tends to undercut the argument that Jesus cannot be more than a prophet. If Jesus was not greater than a prophet, why would all the other respectable figures appear to pay tribute to Jesus? More answers beyond my understanding are required on this, but we know

Jesus himself did say he was more than a prophet (John 4:25–26), and we take him at his word.

Jesus affirmed the scriptural account of Daniel, citing that Daniel was a prophet. "So when you see standing in the holy place 'the abomination that causes desolation,' spoken of through the prophet Daniel" (Matt. 24:15–16). Daniel is recorded in scripture as the man who was thrown into a lion's den overnight for worshiping God against the king's decree, but who escaped unscathed because the lions did not feast on him. "They brought Daniel and threw him into the lions' den. At the first light of dawn, the king got up and hurried to the lions' den. When he came near the den, he called to Daniel in an anguished voice, 'Daniel, has your God, been able to rescue you from the lions?' Daniel answered, 'My God sent his angel, and he shut the mouths of the lions. They have not hurt me'" (Daniel 6:16–17, 19–22).

Jesus cited a scriptural account of David, affirming David and the Law of Moses, when he claimed he is Lord of the Sabbath. "Jesus answered them, 'Have you never read what David did? He entered the house of God, and taking the consecrated bread, he ate what is lawful only for priests to eat.' Then Jesus said to them, 'The Son of Man is Lord of the Sabbath'" (Luke 6:3–5). One of the Ten Commandments by Moses requires observation of the Sabbath day.

Jesus affirmed and cited the scriptural account of Jonah in the belly of a huge fish for three days, and he indicated that this account was a foretelling of his burial for three days in the earth. "For as Jonah was three days and three nights in the belly of a huge fish, so the Son of Man will be three days and three nights in the heart of the earth" (Matt. 12:40). Jonah is one of the minor prophets recorded in scripture as having tried to run away from God after he was instructed to go and prophesy doom to the city of Nineveh. Scriptures say that God sent a huge fish that swallowed and carried Jonah in its belly for three days and night, till it vomited him out in Nineveh. "But the LORD provided a great fish to swallow Jonah, and Jonah was inside the fish three days and three nights" (Jonah 1:17). "And the LORD commanded the fish, and it vomited Jonah onto dry land" (Jonah 2:10).

Jesus affirmed the scripture account of Nineveh, teaching that he is greater than Jonah. "The men of Nineveh will stand up at the judgment with this generation and condemn it; for they repented at the preaching of Jonah" (Matt. 12:41). In this text, Jesus also taught that there will be rising from the death and judgment, and that generations from different points in time will condemn other generations for ignorance.

Jesus affirmed that Jonah was a prophet and taught that those asking for signs today to prove who Jesus is are wicked and adulterous: "He answered, 'A wicked and adulterous generation asks for a sign! But none will be given it except the sign of the prophet Jonah'" (Matt. 12:39).

Jonah's account has also garnered criticism today. This account records Jonah, a prophet of God, was sent to prophesy doom to the city of Nineveh, but he wanted to abdicate this responsibility for many reasons; among them, he felt God was merciful and wouldn't carry out this doom. He probably thought that would be a waste of his time. The account of Jonah tells that God sent a huge fish that swallowed and transported Jonah to Nineveh (Jonah or Jon. 1:17); this account says Jonah was in the belly of the huge fish for three days. Jesus explained that this account of Jonah been in the belly of the huge fish for three days was a foretelling of his burial three day in the earth. This makes this account of Jonah more likely because Jesus later spent three days buried and then resurrected. Jesus predicted his death through this Jonah's account. There is also the miracle of Jesus raising Lazarus from the dead after he was buried for four days (John 11:44). Jesus's teachings are thus very profound, challenging even the best minds today and showing that we cannot just dismiss Jonah's account. Maybe there could be more we haven't learnt yet, so we can't discredit any account in the Bible.

Jesus affirmed the scripture account of Solomon, teaching that Solomon was adorned with splendor: "Consider how the wild flowers grow. Yet I tell you, not even Solomon in all -his splendor was dressed like one of these" (Luke 12:27). Scriptures record that Solomon was one of the kings of Israel, was a son of King David, and was recorded as having been the wisest men who ever lived. "So God said to him … 'I will give you a wise and discerning heart, so that there will never have been anyone like you, nor will there ever be'" (1 Kings 3:11–12).

Jesus affirmed scripture account of Solomon, teaching that there will be rising from the death and judgment. "The Queen of the South will rise at the judgment with this generation and condemn it; for she came from the ends of the earth to listen to Solomon's wisdom, and now something greater than Solomon is here" (Matt. 12:42). Jesus validated the account of Solomon's wisdom but taught that he-Jesus was greater than Solomon.

A couple of things stand out in Jesus's affirmation of Moses's and Jonah's scriptural accounts. Two prophets living many centuries apart foretold of Jesus's death in two very unique ways. Maybe they did not even realize that their actions did this. Jesus says the action of Moses lifting a snake in the wilderness (Numbers or Num. 21:8–9) was prophesying of Jesus's death on the cross. Jonah being in the belly of the huge fish for three days was a foretelling of Jesus's burial (death) for three days. These scriptural accounts uniquely point to the coming Messiah—Jesus and are remarkable.

Jesus is the leader who corroborates and is corroborated by notable respected prophets from other religions.

CHAPTER 5

JESUS TAUGHT
HEAVEN EXISTS

Jesus taught, "No one has ever gone into heaven except the one who came from heaven—the Son of Man" (John 3:13). In this, Jesus claims that heaven is a real place; he had spent time there, he came from heaven, and no one has ever gone to heaven except him.

Jesus further taught that God's house has many rooms, that Jesus is going to prepare a place for people, and that he will come to take people to reside with him there. "My Father's house has many rooms; if that were not so, would I have told you that I am going there to prepare a place for you? And if I go and prepare a place for you, I will come back and take you to be with me" (John 14:2–3).

Jesus indicated he is above all, and that he speaks the words of God and is testifying of the things he has seen and heard from heaven. "The one who comes from heaven is above all. He testifies to what he has seen and heard, but no one accepts his testimony … For the one whom God has sent speaks the words of God" (John 3:31–34).

According to Jesus, no one can see the kingdom of God unless they are born again of water and the Holy Spirit. "Jesus replied, "Very truly I tell you, no one can see the kingdom of God unless they are born again …unless they are born of water and the Spirit" (John 3:3, 5).

Jesus taught and claimed that he learned what he was teaching directly from God, and he has made known to his apostles all this knowledge: "everything that I learned from my Father I have made known to you" (John 15:15). This is why the teachings of Jesus's apostles are valued and accepted. They were at ground zero.

I had a gracious moment of connection or related to Jesus situation, when I had to speak on behalf of my dad when he was detained (family detention). During the time my dad was detained, I spoke and gave testimonies on his behalf about his life and who he is. I found out that I knew my father well to speak on his behalf, and I am sure he's proud I did it. It one day dawned on me that Jesus said he was trying to speak for God. Jesus taught that he was sent by God and that he spoke the words of God (John 3:31–34), which he had learned directly from God (John 15:15). God was and is proud of Jesus's ministry, which was all about God, so I do accept what Jesus said and believe that he was speaking on behalf of God—the father, because I shared and know the passion of one's defense of his dad, especially when your father is misunderstood.

Jesus is the leader who promises a just eternity for all; giving hope to everyone who this earthly life has discriminated against.

CHAPTER 6

JESUS BELIEVED THE HOLY SPIRIT AND HOLY TRINITY

Heightening the importance of the Holy Spirit, Jesus revealed the Holy Trinity in the process. "He breathed on them and said, 'Receive the Holy Spirit. If you forgive anyone's sins, their sins are forgiven; if you do not forgive them, they are not forgiven'" (John 20:21–23). Jesus indicates he has power to forgive sins, was sent by the father, and was sending out and giving his disciples the power to forgive sins.

Jesus revealed the Holy Spirit as the spirit of truth, and he taught that the Holy Spirit will come from the father as an advocate to help and to be with us forever: "And I will ask the Father, and he will give you another advocate to help you and be with you forever, the Spirit of truth" (John 14:16–17). Jesus taught that the Holy Spirit will be sent by God in Jesus's name, and he will play the role of advocacy;

teaching us all things and reminding the disciples everything that Jesus said to them. "But the Advocate, the Holy Spirit, will teach you all things and will remind you of everything I have said to you" (John 14:26). This was an endorsement of the message that the disciples later preached.

Jesus taught that the Holy Spirit will testify about Jesus. Jesus instructed his disciples to testify of him because they were with Jesus from the very beginning: "When the Advocate comes, he will testify about me. And you also must testify, for you have been with me from the beginning" (John 15:26–27). This indicates the Holy Spirit was to come during the lifetime of the disciples to testify of Jesus thus the references by other religions that this text refers to these other religions is not accurate. The Holy Spirit is to guide into all the truth, and he doesn't speak of his own; he speaks only what he hears and will tell of what is yet to come. The Holy Spirit was to glorify Jesus and was to receive from Jesus what he was to make known to the disciples: "But when he, the Spirit of truth, comes, he will guide you into all the truth." (John 16:13–14).

The idea of people speaking by the Holy Spirit today has also garnered criticism and skepticism from modern social culture. This book attempts to speak to this topic of the Holy Spirit: Jesus did reference that David, speaking by the Holy Spirit, prophesied of him

(Mark 12:35–37). Jesus is a trusted authority on this matter, and this indicates that it is not as controversial an issue as it is made out to be. People can be inspired and speak by the Holy Spirit. Jesus is the leader who stands for and affirms unity.

Chapter 7

Jesus Wanted People to Believe in Him

Jesus wanted people to believe in him and he values modern-day believers who have faith in him. He entrusted his disciples to carry his message, and he entrusts his followers today to do the same: "My prayer is not for them alone. I pray also for those who will believe in me through their message" (John 17:20).

Jesus wanted people to believe who he said he was without seeing: "Then Jesus told him, 'Because you have seen me, you have believed; blessed are those who have not seen and yet have believed'" (John 20:29).

Jesus indicated that those who do not believe in him stand condemned. "Whoever believes in him is not condemned, but whoever does not believe stands condemned already" (John 3:18).

Jesus asked people to believe in him equally as God, and he offered that those who do so will perform works Jesus had been doing, and even greater works: "Do not let your hearts be troubled. You believe in God; believe also in me" (John 14:1). "Very truly I tell you, whoever believes in me will do the works I have been doing, and they will do even greater things than these" (John 14:12).

Jesus taught that loving him is keeping his commands, and he claimed these words were from God: "Whoever has my commands and keeps them is the one who loves me. Jesus replied, 'Anyone who loves me will obey my teaching. Anyone who does not love me will not obey my teaching. These words you hear are not my own; they belong to the Father who sent me'" (John 14:21, 23–24).

Jesus indicated that he was going to be lifted up on the cross, and that those who will believe in him will have eternal life: "that everyone who believes may have eternal life in him" (John 3:15). Jesus explained eternal life as knowing the only true God and Jesus Christ, whom God sent: "Now this is eternal life: that they know you, the only true God, and Jesus Christ, whom you have sent" (John 17:3).

Jesus taught he is the vine anyone needs to remain connected to in order to bear fruits, and that bearing much fruit shows one is his disciple: "Remain in me, as I also remain in you. Neither can you bear fruit unless you remain in me" (John 15:4). "This is to my Father's glory, that you bear much fruit, showing yourselves to be my disciples" (John 15:8).

Jesus promised that for those who remain in him, and Jesus's words remain in them, they can ask and will receive whatever they wish: "if you remain in me and my words remain in you, ask whatever you wish, and it will be done for you" (John 15:7). Jesus indicated that whoever rejects him will not see life: "whoever believes in the Son has eternal life, but whoever rejects the Son will not see life" (John 3:36).

The notion or view that there is only one way to God or to heaven—as Jesus put it, he is the way, the truth, and the life—has also been challenged by other religions. With all due respect, other religions appear to promise good things and prescribe that followers should live a morally upright and peaceful life, and all will be well in the end. These are good and noble promises and actions, yet scriptures (and prophet Isaiah) appear to undercut these other religions points of view. Prophet Isaiah says that Jesus is the prince of peace (Isaiah or Isa. 9:6). Jesus is introduced as the pinnacle of peace. No other religion has been able to claim supremacy over Jesus's teachings. Jesus said that he has been tasked to die for the sins of all mankind. God would not allow his son to die for humanity if God was not trying to support his son's claim that Jesus is the way, the truth, and the life, and that no one comes to the father except through Jesus. No one and no religion has been able to disprove Jesus's claim to be the only way; they are all unsubstantiated.

Jesus did not compel the people of his days to follow him; in fact, we know that the religious leaders insisted he must die because he claimed to be the son of God (John 19:7). What we know is that Jesus wanted to distinguish himself from the religion that was practiced in his day, in the name of God. Jesus did not disrespectfully show his points of differences with these religious practices. These practices that we know were in contrast with what he wanted, and now we know he was right. He referred to some Pharisees and teachers of the law as hypocrites (Matt. 15:1–7). Taking cues from Jesus, it is thus okay to contrast Jesus and the other religions. We know today that Jesus claimed to be Lord, and by connecting that with the fact that the Ten Commandments (which Jesus indicated were from God) were not been followed, we can conclude that he demonstrated great humility and religious tolerance. Jesus was restrained in highlighting these differences between him and other religious practices, refusing to use his authority and power to condemn. This sets the model for today's religious differences and dialogues. Contrasting religions in a restrained manner is part of religious tolerance.

Jesus is the leader who was and is not pre-occupied finding a successor, not pre-occupied forcing others to follow him, not pre-occupied forcing unbelievers to submit, not pre-occupied chasing legacy or history, but who built and builds legacy and made history by laying down his life out of love for others.

CHAPTER 8

JESUS BELIEVED AND AFFIRMED THE CREATION ACCOUNT

The creation account is recorded in Genesis 1:1–31; 2:1–25. This account details that God created everything in six days. Mankind is reported as having been created on the sixth day. The Genesis account details that God created heaven, the earth, light, the sky, the sun, the moon, and all living creatures; he also separated the waters and the dry ground. The account says God rested on the seven day, blessing it to be holy.

Jesus showed that this creation account, where man was created from mud, is not strange or far-fetched as modern social culture and evolutionist would like to make it. Jesus healed a blind man by applying mud to his eyes (John 9:6–7). Jesus is recorded as spitting on the ground to create mud, and applying the mud to the blind man's eyes to heal him, showing that humans or eyes can be created and formed from mud by God; we therefore cannot dismiss this creation account.

Jesus indicated that the world came after him and God. "And now, Father, glorify me in your presence with the glory I had with you before the world began" (John 17:5). He confirmed the world was created: "Father, I want those you have given me to be with me where I am, and to see my glory, the glory you have given me because you loved me before the creation of the world" (John 17:24). Jesus supported and affirmed the creation account: "But at the beginning of creation God made them male and female" (Mark 10:6–9).

Solomon, one of the wisest men who ever lived, collaborated and affirmed the creation account with Jesus. Solomon indicates God made the earth, set the heaven in place, gave the sea its boundary and marked out the foundation of the earth.

> "I, wisdom, was appointed from eternity, from the beginning, before the world began. When there were no oceans, I was given birth, when there were no springs abounding with water; before the mountains were settled in place, before the hills, I was given birth, before he made the earth or its fields or any of the dust of the world. I was there when he set the heavens in place, when he marked out the horizon on the face of the deep, when he established the clouds above and fixed securely the fountains

of the deep, when he gave the sea its boundary so the waters would not overstep his command, and when he marked out the foundations of the earth" (Proverbs or Prov. 8:12, 22–30).

In a conversation with Job, God claimed creation, indicating he laid the foundation of the earth, marked its dimension, set its footing, laid its cornerstone, and created the behemoth and men.

"Where were you when I laid the earth's foundation? Who marked off its dimensions? Who stretched a measuring line across it? On what were its footings set, or who laid its cornerstone while the morning stars sang together and all the angels shouted for joy? "Who shut up the sea behind doors when it burst forth from the womb, when I made the clouds its garment and wrapped it in thick darkness, when I fixed limits for it and set its doors and bars in place? ... Look at Behemoth, which I made along with you. It ranks first among the works of God" (Job 38:4–11; 40:15, 19). In this exchange, God claims everything under heaven belongs to him (Job 41:11). This account also speaks to atheists (those who believe there is no God). God asks if those who contends with him can correct him, and if they would condemn God to justify themselves (Job 40:2, 8). Scriptures says that the fools says in their heart there is no God (Psalms 14:1).

Jesus is the leader who upholds creation.

Chapter 9

Jesus Believed the Ten Commandment and Commanded People to Love and to Be Merciful

Jesus affirmed, believed, and quoted some of the Ten Commandments. Jesus inferred that observing the Ten Commandments is part of inheriting eternal life.

> A man ran up to him and fell on his knees before him. "Good teacher," he asked, "what must I do to inherit eternal life?" Jesus answered. "You know the commandments: 'You shall not murder, you shall not commit adultery, you shall not steal, you shall not give false testimony, you shall not defraud, honor your father and mother.'" (Mark 10:17–19).

The Ten Commandments

1. "You shall have no other gods before me." (Exodus or Exod. 20:3)

2. "You shall not make for yourself an idol." (Exod. 20:4–6)

3. "You shall not misuse the name of the LORD your God." (Exod. 20:7)

4. "Remember the Sabbath day by keeping it holy." (Exod. 20:8–11)

5. "Honor your father and your mother." (Exod. 20:12)

6. "You shall not murder." (Exod. 20:13)

7. "You shall not commit adultery." (Exod. 20:14)

8. "You shall not steal." (Exod. 20:15)

9. "You shall not give false testimony against your neighbor." (Exod. 20:16)

10. "You shall not covet your neighbor's house." (Exod. 20:17)

Jesus indicated that the Ten Commandments were from God. Jesus added, "For God said, 'Honor your father and mother'" (Matt. 15:1–7). Jesus was in the process of explaining the prophet Isaiah.

Jesus taught and quoted the Ten Commandments, and he explained the greatest commandment of all. "The most important one," answered Jesus, "is this: 'Hear, O Israel: The Lord our God, the Lord is one. Love the Lord your God with all your heart and with all your soul and with all your mind and with all your strength.' The second is this: 'Love your neighbor as yourself.' There is no commandment greater than these." (Mark 12:29–31).

Jesus indicated his command to us is that people should Love each other as he has loved, by laying down his life. Jesus explained that his friends are those who obey his command: "Greater love has no one than this: to lay down one's life for one's friends. You are my friends if you do what I command" (John 15:12–14). "This is my command: Love each other" (John 15:17). Jesus indicated that keeping his commands is the proof of loving him: "If you love me, keep my commands" (John 14:15).

Jesus taught that those who love him are those who keep and obey his commands. He explains that these words are from God: "Whoever has my commands and keeps them is the one who loves me. Jesus replied, 'Anyone who loves me will obey my teaching. These words you hear are not my own; they belong to the Father who sent me'" (John 14: 21, 23–24).

No human constitution or law can be perfect as human beings are not perfect. Scripture indicates that the lord is known for his acts of justice (Psalms 9:16). Jesus inferred the Ten Commandments are from God. It might then be agreeable to promote the Ten Commandments equally as the constitution to support the banners 'One Nation under God', 'in God we Trust', 'so help me God' oath or a Nation Anthem lyric 'Oh God of all Creation'. The Law of the Lord is perfect (Psalms 19:7).

The wisdom call or cry that we aim our legality/ legal decisions, values and moral standards to the sun so if we miss we land on the moon, asks everyone to set as the standard, adhere, aspire, have as the goal or aim to obey God's law - (which is perfect and of a higher standard) - as this will only help in being able to obey, adhere or follow the law and constitution written by men. Jesus: "What good will it be for someone to gain the whole world, yet forfeit their soul?" (Mathew 16:26).

CHAPTER 10

JESUS TAUGHT DIVORCE IS BREAKING A COMMANDMENT

Jesus taught that divorce is breaking a commandment and committing adultery. "He answered, 'Anyone who divorces his wife and marries another woman commits adultery against her. And if she divorces her husband and marries another man, she commits adultery'" (Mark 10:10–12). The people must have been misusing marriage, divorcing for no reason may be. I don't know. Their hearts were hard (Mark 10:5)

Changing water to wine was the first of Jesus's miraculous signs, which he performed at Cana in Galilee wedding. This sends a message, although inadvertently, that marriage must be important.

"Jesus and his disciples had also been invited to the wedding. When the wine was gone; Jesus said to the servants, "Fill the jars with water"; so they filled them to the brim. Then he told them, "Now draw some out and take it to the master of the banquet." They did so, and the master of the banquet tasted the water that had been turned into wine. This, the first of his miraculous signs, Jesus performed at Cana in Galilee" (John 2:1–11).

At thirty years of age when Jesus began his ministry (Luke 3:23), he was not married. He was still unmarried almost three years later at his death. Jesus is the leader who relates and consoles.

CHAPTER 11

JESUS AFFIRMED THE
SANCTITY OF LIFE AND
AFFIRMED THAT BABIES
IN THE WOMB HAVE
LIFE AND FEELINGS

Jesus affirmed and validated that the unborn have feelings of joy and have life. This goes against abortion advocates. In a Bible account where Mary was pregnant with Jesus, it is recorded that as soon as Mary greeted her cousin Elizabeth, who was also pregnant with John the Baptist, the baby in Elizabeth's womb leaped in her womb for joy on recognizing Jesus in Mary's womb. "When Elizabeth heard Mary's greeting, the baby leaped in her womb, and Elizabeth was filled with the Holy Spirit. As soon as the sound of your greeting reached my ears, the baby in my womb leaped for joy" (Luke 1:39–41, 44).

Jesus later taught that the unborn are children who bring joy, and he implied that the unborn are not to be aborted. "A woman giving birth to a child has pain because her time has come; but when her baby is born she forgets the anguish because of her joy that a child is born into the world" (John 16:21).

Scriptures in Genesis 25:21-26, supports Jesus and the facts that fetuses or unborn babies in the womb are people or human beings. In this Genesis 25:21-26 scripture excerpt, God called and explained the jostling of the twin brothers Jacob and Esau, who were in Rebekah's womb as 'two people' and 'two nations'. The two unborn babies, Jacob and Esau in Rebekah's womb, jostled each other in her womb. God explained this jostling as the older will serve the younger. Jostling (elbowing or pushing) each other in an effort to re-position is a human characteristic. At their birth, baby Jacob came out with his hand grasping his twin brother baby Esau's heels. This led to him (baby Jacob) been named or given the name Jacob which means 'he grasped/held the heel'. Jacob later became known as the modern day Israel. Grasping someone in an effort to slow down or overtake is a human characteristic; proving yet again fetuses or unborn babies in the womb are human beings jostling or grasping the other. God calls unborn babies "two nations are in your womb" (Genesis 25:23).

At the second trimester, the unborn baby John just sixth months in Elizabeth's womb (Luke 1:36), had the human feeling of joy. At the first trimester, the unborn baby Jesus just a few weeks in Mary's womb, had the human ability to communicate or inspire the human feeling of joy to yet another unborn baby john. It goes without saying that the unborn babies in the wombs are human beings. Unborn lives matter. Unborn lives deserve the human right to choose life. Unborn lives deserve due process. Unborn lives need a voice. Jesus is the leader who advocates for the unborn. Jesus is the leader who respects life.

CHAPTER 12

JESUS BELIEVED IN PRAYERS, TAUGHT HOW TO PRAY, AND WANT PEOPLE TO PRAY

Jesus taught how to pray. The Lord's Prayer says, "Our Father in heaven, hallowed be your name, your kingdom come, your will be done, on earth as it is in heaven. Give us today our daily bread. And forgive us our debts, as we also have forgiven our debtors. And lead us not into temptation, but deliver us from the evil one" (Matt. 6:9–15). Jesus indicated that God in heaven forgives sin and debts, and he expects men to do likewise and forgive each other. Jesus also affirmed the existences of heaven and taught that for those who forgive other people when they sin against them, God will most likely forgive them.

Jesus instructed people to ask anything in his name. "And I will do whatever you ask in my name … You may ask me for anything in my name, and I will do it" (John 14:13–14). Jesus promised he would do this so that the father may be glorified in the son.

Jesus taught that God will give out whatever is asked in his name, and he instructed people to ask, promising that they will receive so that their joy may be complete. "Very truly I tell you, my Father will give you whatever you ask in my name" (John 16:23–24). This is one of the reasons why people ask prayers in Jesus's name.

Jesus taught that with God, all things are possible. "Jesus looked at them and said, 'All things are possible with God'" (Mark 10:27). This is why people should have confidence in God.

The mention of 'give us today our daily bread' in the Lord's Prayer, appear to indicate Jesus want people to pray daily. Jesus is the leader who offers solutions, meets and wants to meet the needs of everyone. Jesus is the leader who forgives sins. Jesus is the leader who is accessible.

CHAPTER 13

JESUS TAUGHT THAT EVIL SPIRITS EXIST AND OFFERED INSIGHTS ON HOW EVIL SPIRITS OPERATE TO RUIN PEOPLE'S LIVES

J esus indicated that he had knowledge of the dark, or the underground, when he described the operation of evil spirit. He taught that evil spirits exists and are wicked:

> "When an impure spirit comes out of a person, it goes through arid places seeking rest and does not find it. Then it says, "I will return to the house I left." When it arrives, it finds the house unoccupied, swept clean and put in order. Then it goes and takes with it seven other spirits more wicked than itself, and they go in and live there. And the final condition

of that person is worse than the first" (Matt. 12:43–45).

Jesus had a back-and-forth conversation with some impure spirits who had recognized him as the son of God. They expressed fear Jesus wound torture them:

"A man with an impure spirit came from the tombs to meet him. When he saw Jesus from a distance, he ran and fell on his knees in front of him. He shouted at the top of his voice, "What do you want with me, Jesus, Son of the Most High God? In God's name don't torture me!" For Jesus had said to him, "Come out of this man, you impure spirit!" Then Jesus asked him, "What is your name?" "My name is Legion," he replied, "for we are many" (Mark 5:1–10).

This encounter revealed that impure spirits have life and were aware of who Jesus was. The impure spirits have a way to subdue, control, speak, and inhabit a person, which is not a good thing. Evil spirits are not mankind's friends.

Jesus taught that a prince of this world is coming. Jesus's use of the metaphor prince infers that the prince of this world has power or influence: "The prince of this world is coming. He comes so that the world may learn that I love the Father and do exactly what my Father has commanded me" (John 14:30–31). Jesus is not friends with this prince, because he is saying that the prince of this world has no hold on him. Jesus indicates that the coming of the prince of this world only helps to reveal Jesus's obedience and love for God.

Jesus taught that he witnessed Satan fall from heaven like lightning. Jesus thus affirmed the existence of Satan and heaven. He indicated that Satan and evil spirits are enemies of mankind and are deadly as snakes and scorpions. "He replied, 'I saw Satan fall like lightning from heaven. However, do not rejoice that the spirits submit to you, but rejoice that your names are written in heaven'" (Luke 10:18–20). In this text, Jesus also revealed that names are written in heaven.

The Book of Jude collaborates Jesus's message of the existence of Satan and fallen angels. "And the angels who did not keep their positions of authority but abandoned their proper dwelling—these he has kept in darkness, bound with everlasting chains for judgment on the great Day" (Jude 1:6). Jude also refers to the angel Michael as Archangel Michael. Archangel Michael is said to be disputing with the devil about the body of Moses: "But even the archangel Michael, when he was disputing with the devil about the body of Moses, did not himself dare to condemn him for slander but said, 'The Lord rebuke you!'" (Jude 1:9). This mention of Archangel Michael exercising care in dealing with the devil offers insight that the devil is not to be underestimated. The revelation here, that the devil uses slander (makes false and damaging statements about someone), should caution everyone as to the nature and kinds of attacks to expect from the devil—the father of all lies (John 8:44).

The existence of violence today sure appears to confirm that evil does exist. The extreme censorship, smear, intimidations, dirty politics, propaganda and spin used by corrupt power hungry politicians, corrupt political parties, corrupt presidents/leaders, corrupt governments or dishonest media to hide or cover up evil, failed or bad policies are forms of lies indicating how people engage in slander or how people can be deceived or how message can be distorted to protect the guilty and hidden agendas. When truth is discovered it might be too late. People go into hiding when the evil are in power (Proverbs 28:28). Hiding can be literally as exemplified by terrorist strong holds or can be manifested in the lack of free speech, lack of transparency, extreme censorship etc. When a country is led by a leader who lacks discernment and knowledge there is turmoil, scandals or lack of order (Proverbs 28:2).

Jesus is the leader with knowledge and discernment. Jesus is the leader who tells the truth. Jesus's leadership is all about helping people. Jesus is the leader who looks out for the folks.

CHAPTER 14

JESUS TAUGHT THAT THE WORLD WILL COME TO AN END, AND HE TAUGHT OF HIS SECOND COMING

Jesus taught that there will be an end to all this life: "And this gospel of the kingdom will be preached in the whole world as a testimony to all nations, and then the end will come" (Matt. 24:14). Jesus indicated that the gospel of the kingdom, as a testimony, will first be preached to all nations before the end comes (Mark 13:10).

Jesus taught that his second coming will be coming in clouds with great power and glory: "At that time people will see the Son of Man coming in clouds with great power and glory. Heaven and earth will pass away, but my words will never pass away" (Mark 13:24–27, 31). Jesus establishes supremacy when he indicates that heaven and earth will pass away, but his word will never pass. Again, he indicates "the sun will be darkened, and the moon will not give its light; the stars will fall from the sky, and the heavenly bodies will be shaken." This goes against all those who advocate the worship of the earth as Mother Earth.

Jesus is the leader who helps and wants to save all.

CHAPTER 15

JESUS DID NOT CONDONE SEXUAL IMMORALITY AND TAUGHT THAT THERE WILL BE A JUDGMENT DAY AND AFTERLIFE

Jesus quoted the scriptural account of the cities of Sodom and Gomorrah to affirm Judgment Day and afterlife. These two cities were destroyed by fire raining down from the sky because of their sins. Jesus taught that it will be more bearable for the inhabitants of these two cities on the Day of Judgment: "If anyone will not welcome you or listen to your words, leave that home or town and shake the dust off your feet. Truly I tell you, it will be more bearable for Sodom and Gomorrah on the Day of Judgment than for that town" (Matt. 10:14–15). Jesus did not condone sexual immorality or sexual perversion because he indicated that it will be more bearable for the cities of Sodom

and Gomorrah on the Day of Judgment. Sodom
and Gomorrah were destroyed by fire raining down
from the sky. Two whole cities were destroyed by fire
raining down from the sky, and that is not a simple
punishment. Yet Jesus is saying that it will be more
bearable for Sodom and Gomorrah than those who
reject Jesus's message ("if anyone will not welcome
you or listen to your words").

What do we know about Sodom and Gomorrah?
Jude's scriptural account claims that sexual immorality
and perversion was a factor in the destruction of
Sodom and Gomorrah, and that this was an example
of eternal fire punishment. "In a similar way, Sodom
and Gomorrah and the surrounding towns gave
themselves up to sexual immorality and perversion.
They serve as an example of those who suffer the
punishment of eternal fire" (Jude 1:7).

Scripture accounts of the city of Sodom in Genesis
mention homosexual desire by the men of Sodom
towards Lot's male visitors. Lot is recorded as calling
these requests for sexual advances wicked. Lot tries
to give the men of the city of Sodom his daughters
instead.

> "Before they had gone to bed, all the men from
> every part of the city of Sodom—both young
> and old—surrounded the house. They called
> to Lot, "Where are the men who came to you
> tonight? Bring them out to us so that we can

have sex with them." Lot went outside to meet them and shut the door behind him and said, "No, my friends. Don't do this wicked thing. Look, I have two daughters who have never slept with a man. Let me bring them out to you, and you can do what you like with them." (Gen. 19:3–8).

Merriam-Webster's Dictionary defines Gomorrah as "a place notorious for vice (example sexual immorality) and corruption." Urban Dictionary has an even more explicit sexual definition. The word Sodom rhymes with the dictionary word sodomy. People against homosexuality have argued that the use of the words Gomorrah and Sodom, when tied to the scriptural account of Jude, leave no doubt as to the implied meaning. Lot, who knew his city and its morals better than us, called homosexual advances wicked. Lot didn't use the words "aggressive" or "disrespectful," and he didn't think offering his daughters for sex to an "aggressive" mob was wicked. Jesus did not offer a correction to Lot's words. Jesus did not like the sexual immorality or sexual perversion practiced in Sodom and Gomorrah, but according to Jesus, it will be more bearable for Sodom and Gomorrah than those who reject Jesus's message. Jesus referenced marriage between a man and a woman (Mark 10:10-12).

Jesus would not endorse sin, wickedness, perversion or some of the things practiced in Sodom and Gomorrah that will be 'more bearable'. Jesus would not discriminate either. Whatever Jesus would do or not do, could be the guiding principle to helping resolve any of today's hot button social cultural issue. Jesus is the leader who loves everyone.

CHAPTER 16

JESUS WARNED OF FALSE PROPHETS AND WARNED OF PERSECUTIONS OF HIS FOLLOWERS

Jesus foresaw and warned that his disciples would die cruel deaths. History has affirmed this because all of Jesus's disciples (other than John and Judas Iscariot) died a martyr's death (tortured and killed for preaching Jesus's message). Even John suffered for the message of Jesus: "Jesus said to them, "You will drink the cup I drink and be baptized with the baptism I am baptized with, but to sit at my right or left is not for me to grant" (Mark10:39–40). In this text, Jesus also revealed that there will be a left and right sitting in Jesus's future.

These are the names of Jesus's twelve disciples, per Mathew 10:2–4.

1. Simon (who is called Peter)
2. Simon's brother Andrew

3. James, son of Zebedee
4. James's brother John
5. Philip
6. Bartholomew
7. Thomas
8. Matthew, the tax collector
9. James, son of Alphaeus
10. Thaddaeus
11. Simon the Zealot
12. Judas Iscariot, who betrayed Jesus. Judas was later substituted.

Jesus warned that people will kill his followers in the future, in the name of offering service to God. Jesus warned that these people will do this because they are misinformed and misguided about who God or Jesus is. "They will put you out of the synagogue; in fact, the time is coming when anyone who kills you will think they are offering a service to God. They will do such things because they have not known the Father or me" (John 16:2–3). Christians have been targeted and beheaded by terrorists all over the world, bringing to light Jesus's warning. Christian's persecutions are used to deter or stop more people from openly following Jesus.

Jesus did not ask his followers to harm or kill people. This is a sharp contrast to religious-driven terrorist acts today. "Jesus commanded Peter, 'Put your sword away!'" (John 18:11). "When the disciples

James and John saw this, they asked, 'Lord, do you want us to call fire down from heaven to destroy them even as Elijah did?' But Jesus turned and rebuked them And he said, 'You do not know what kind of spirit you are of, for the Son of Man did not come to destroy men's lives, but to save them'" (Luke 9:54–55). Terrorists who claim killing other people is part of their religion and who are following the message of a prophet should also adhere to the peaceful, nonviolent message of Jesus the prophet. Jesus commanded his followers to love and be merciful to others, including enemies.

Jesus indicated that marriage is for the people of this age and that there are no marriages in heaven. "Jesus replied, 'The people of this age marry and are given in marriage. But those who are considered worthy of taking part in the age to come and in the resurrection from the dead will neither marry nor be given in marriage' (Luke 20:34–36). The promises that there will be virgins waiting to be a reward to those who die while conducting terror is not true according to Jesus.

Jesus warned of false prophets and messiahs appearing, and he warned against people following signs and wonders other than him. "For false messiahs and false prophets will appear and perform signs and wonders to deceive, if possible, even the elect" (Mark 13:22). Jesus warned against following these signs or these prophets; it implies that the agenda of those misleading Jesus's followers must not be good. Jesus wanted people to follow him alone. The Bible is the only literature that indicates prophets performing many signs and wonders; thus those seeking signs and prophets should look to the Bible as the touchstone.

Jesus taught that everyone who does evil hate the light for they fear been exposed. "Everyone who does evil hates the light, and will not come into the light for fear that their deeds will be exposed" (John 3:19–21).

It is plausible as Jesus warned, for false prophets to appear and deceive. A false prophet has a lying temperament; can't hold to the truth as lying is the native language (John 8:44). The attempts by secular culture or some religions to trivialize the bible and the false mischaracterization or minimization of Jesus can be interpreted by Jesus's followers as efforts to hide the truth, hide the light or deceive. After all Jesus is the one who warned this would happen. The standard as Jesus set it, of a true prophet or a true leader, should not be empty rhetoric's message or speech, but should be that they lay down their life out of love for others in order to get power or get a following. Jesus is the true leader and prophet who leads and led by laying down his life out of love for all.

CHAPTER 17

IMPORTANT TO KNOW: WIDELY QUOTED SOCIAL AND CULTURAL MAXIMS OF JESUS

On a pure academic and originality basis, Jesus is not given all the credit he's due. We know that Jesus is the originator of phrases like "do to others what you would have them do to you" (Matt. 7:12) and other widely quoted social cultural maxims, such as the sayings below.

1. "Love your enemies, do good to those who hate you, bless those who curse you, pray for those who mistreat you" (Luke 6:27–28).
2. "If someone slaps you on one cheek, turn to them the other also" (Luke 6:29).
3. "Give to everyone who asks you" (Luke 6:30).
4. "Do to others as you would have them do to you" (Luke 6:31).

5. "Love your enemies, do good to them" (Luke 6:35).

6. "Be merciful, just as your Father is merciful" (Luke 6:36). Jesus reveals the character of God as merciful, and he instructed mankind to emulate God and be merciful to one another.

7. "Do not judge and you will not be judged" (Luke 6:37).

8. "Give and it will be given to you" (Luke 6:38).

9. "Pay attention to the plank in your own eye not the speck of sawdust in your brother's eye" (Luke 6:41).

The influence of these maxims, and even the Lord's Prayer, is far-reaching and beyond any academic and scholarly publication. Some of these maxims are universally quoted and have formed the basis of many universal morals and values across many religions, nations and cultures. The Nobel Prize award or other prize awards wouldn't do them enough justice.

Jesus is the leader who inspires generations with extraordinary wisdom and knowledge.

CHAPTER 18

BIBLE DISCLOSURE AND CONCLUSION

The Bible

"The Bible is a collection of scriptures written at different times by different authors in different locations. Jews and Christians consider the books of the Bible to be a product of divine inspiration or an authoritative record of the relationship between God and humans."[1]

It took about 1,500 years for the whole Bible to be written—from Genesis, written at the time of Moses, to Revelation, written by the apostle John about 65 years after Jesus' death. The Bible has two major parts—the Old Testament and the New Testament. The Old Testament is a collection of 39 books. Both Jews and Christians accept these books as Scripture.

---

[1] Wikipedia, "Bible," accessed May 14, 2016.

The New Testament is made up of 27 books accepted by Christians as Scripture. The Old Testament was first written in the Hebrew and Aramaic languages. About 250 years before Jesus' birth, it was translated into Greek (this text was called the Septuagint). All of the New Testament was written in Greek.[2]

Many have pointed to Jesus's quoted scriptures, thus validating and confirming that scriptures are inspired and divine. On occasion Jesus quoted from the Torah, also known as the "five books of Moses" (Genesis, Exodus, Leviticus, Numbers, and Deuteronomy), thus validating Moses. In Exodus, Moses is recorded as speaking with God in front of several hundred or thousand eyewitnesses, affirming for many that the scriptures are divine and God given: "Then Moses led the people out of the camp to meet with God" (Exod. 19:17–19). "When the people saw the thunder and lightning and heard the trumpet and saw the mountain in smoke, they trembled with fear. They stayed at a distance and said to Moses, 'Speak to us yourself and we will listen. But do not have God speak to us or we will die'" (Exod. 20:18–19).

No one has found any errors or inconsistency in the scriptures. This consistency in scriptures, written

---

[2] The Holy Bible: New International Version, "About the Bible," page v.

by different authors at different locations over a period spanning one thousand years yet with a similar message or theme, leads to the conclusion that the scriptures are divine and inspired.

Many modern Protestants point to the following four "Criteria for Canonicity" to justify the selection of the books that have been included in the New Testament.

1. Apostolic Origin—attributed to and based upon the preaching and teaching of the first-generation apostles (or their close companions).

2. Universal Acceptance—acknowledged by all major Christian communities in the ancient world (by the end of the fourth century) as well as accepted canon by Jewish authorities (for the Old Testament).

3. Liturgical Use—read publicly when early Christian communities gathered for the Lord's Supper (their weekly worship services).

4. Consistent Message—containing a theological outlook similar to or complementary to other accepted Christian writings.[3]

There are four canonical gospels in the Bible. These four gospels (Matthew, Mark, Luke, and John) document in detail the life of Jesus.

---

[3] Wikipedia. "Biblical Canon," accessed May 14, 2016.

Modern scholars have concluded that the Canonical Gospels went through four stages in their formation.

1. The first stage was oral, and included various stories about Jesus such as healing the sick, or debating with opponents, as well as parables and teachings.

2. In the second stage, the oral traditions began to be written down in collections (collections of miracles, collections of sayings, etc.), while the oral traditions continued to circulate

3. In the third stage, early Christians began combining the written collections and oral traditions into what might be called "proto-gospels" – hence Luke's reference to the existence of "many" earlier narratives about Jesus

4. In the fourth stage, the authors of our four Gospels drew on these proto-gospels, collections, and still-circulating oral traditions to produce the gospels of Matthew, Mark, Luke and John.[4]

There are other extra or non-biblical accounts on Jesus, such as the works of first-century Roman-Jewish historian Flavius Josephus, which this book did

[4] Wikipedia. "Oral Gospel Traditions," accessed May 14, 2016.

not explore or vet. According to Wikipedia, Flavius Josephus was a first-century historian who lived a few years after Jesus's death. His account, recorded in the antiquities of the Jews, appears to support and affirm the biblical accounts. Flavius Josephus writes that Jesus was an extraordinary person of his day, and he was referred to as Christ. Flavius Josephus's account cannot be accused of bias because he had no religious proselytizing goals as a historian and independent Bible collaborator. Some religions have tried to argue the Bible's account of Jesus could have had bias in that regard. Flavius Josephus would have had the opportunity to check the veracity of the circulating accounts of Jesus before writing his account for his credibility. However, this book has relied on the biblical and scriptural account of Jesus and recommend the Bible for any extra reading on Jesus.

Summing up, we all know of people who have not done as they say. Some prominent religions and religious figures have even asked people to follow what they say and not what they do. On the other hand, Jesus appears to practice what he teaches. Jesus teaches that greater love has no one than this: to lay down one's life for one's friends (John 15:12–14). Jesus later gave his life for many for the forgiveness of sins (Matt. 26:26–28). He teaches that people should forgive or be merciful just as God is merciful. It will be more bearable for the inhabitants of the cities of Sodom and Gomorrah on the Day of Judgment (Matt. 10:14–15)—cities that we know gave themselves up to sexual immorality and perversion (Jude 1:7). Jesus taught and coined the phrase "judge not, and you shall not be judge," and he lived up to his teachings. Jesus accepted everyone the way they were. Jesus did not condemn an adulterer (John 8:1–11) condemned for death by stoning and brought to Jesus to support the stoning sentence. Jesus asked everyone to look and judge their own hearts and lives; if they were not sinners, they could cast the first stone. No one wanted to be at the mercy of other people's personal evaluations and assessments, but Jesus knew their hearts and outcome—that's fair justice. There are some in the Christian faith, inadvertently or maybe with good intentions, who have caused misinformation and misrepresentation of Jesus through churches and religious separations. No one human being can fully represent Jesus, and thus there's no need for other people to compare themselves with others' spirituality. No one can measure up to Jesus. Jesus's death was to help bridge the gap between humanity and God (John 3:16). Jesus knew all this and exercised due diligence sua sponte for our benefit in addressing some of these hot topics of today. creation, existence of God, existence of heaven, the Holy Spirit, existence of Satan and evil spirits, the Bible, marriage, babies in the womb, the Ten Commandments, Noah's account of the flood, Jonah being transported in the belly of a large fish to Nineveh, and more.

I hope this book was able to speak to these following seminal teachings of Jesus.

- Jesus taught he was Lord,
- Jesus taught that he is the son of God, Christ, the messiah, and the savior of the world. He is more than a prophet
- Jesus believed, affirmed, and quoted scriptures (the Bible).
- Jesus taught that heaven exists.
- Jesus believed in the Holy Spirit and the Holy Trinity.
- Jesus wanted people to believe in him.
- Jesus believed and affirmed the creation account.
- Jesus believed the Ten Commandments and commanded people to love and be merciful.
- Jesus taught divorce is breaking a commandment.
- Jesus affirmed the sanctity of life and affirmed that babies in the womb have life and feelings.
- Jesus believed in prayers, taught how to pray, and want people to pray.
- Jesus taught that evil spirit exists and gave insights on how evil spirits operate to ruin people's lives.

- Jesus taught that the world will come to an end, and he taught of his second coming.
- Jesus did not condone sexual immorality and taught that there will be a Judgment Day and afterlife.
- Jesus warned of false prophets and warned of persecution of his followers.
- And highlighted important to know widely quoted social cultural maxims of Jesus.

In conclusion, "Jesus did many other things as well. If every one of them were written down, I suppose that even the whole world would not have room for the books that would be written" (John 21:25). This preview book is just my perspective, and it should not take priority over or foreclose others. There are many reasons as highlighted to Learn from, be a disciple of or follow Jesus.

NOTES ABOUT THE AUTHOR

Isaac Kinuthia has no theological education, training, or background. He is a professional licensed civil engineer in Michigan and Wisconsin. Isaac recommends reading the Bible to learn more about Jesus. Isaac grew up and obtained his high school education in Kiambu Kenya. Isaac holds a bachelor of science in civil engineering from Michigan Technological University. This book was written to test fulfilling, supplementing, or proving EB1 requirements. This book also helps to record what Isaac tried to follow regarding Jesus while growing up in Kiambu Kenya.

CPSIA information can be obtained at www.ICGtesting.com
Printed in the USA
BVOW02s0454300916

463789BV00001B/4/P